THE
DIVA CODE

THE
DIVA CODE

MISS PIGGY on Life, Love, and the
10,000 Idiotic Things ~~Men~~ Do
FROGS

by

Miss Piggy

AS TOLD TO JIM LEWIS

HYPERION

NEW YORK

Library of Congress Cataloging-in-Publication Data
Lewis, Jim, 1952–
The diva code : Miss Piggy on life, love, and the 10,000 idiotic
things men frogs do / by Miss Piggy as told to Jim Lewis.
p. cm.
ISBN 978-1-4013-2316-5
1. Conduct of life—Humor. 2. Man-woman
relationships—Humor. I. Title.
PN6231.C6142L47 2009
818'.5402—dc22   2008026523

Hyperion books are available for special promotions, premiums, or corporate training.
For details contact Michael Rentas, Proprietary Markets, Hyperion, 77 West 66th Street,
12th floor, New York, New York 10023, or call 212-456-0133.

Design by Pauline Neuwirth, Neuwirth & Associates, Inc.

FIRST EDITION

10 9 8 7 6 5 4 3 2 1

· CONTENTS ·

Speaking of the Diva

'Tis moi!

And here, at long last, is moi's new book! (Relax, it's not another celebrity children's book about *Flinky the Happy Plumbing Elf* or some such.) Au contraire, this is a book of moi's insights on love, men, frogs, beauty, fashion, attitude, wealth, health, and being a diva. This is *the* book for anyone who has ever dreamed of living more like moi. And frankly, who hasn't had *that* dream, n'est pas?

Over the years, moi has gleaned, glommed, and garnered much wisdom about what's wrong with everyone else and what's right with moi. But, until now, sharing this wisdom seemed so futile. After all, I've been telling my many celebrity friends how to live *their* lives for years, but few of them ever took my advice. (Wonder what happens to folks who don't listen to moi? Just watch one of those *Excess Celebrity* entertainment shows. One minute you're a star, the next all your 8x10s are mug shots.)

Then it hit me: People! Not celebrities, but actual real-world not-yet-had-their-fifteen-minutes-of-fame people—like vous—would *love* to learn what moi knows about men, frogs, and everything else! And all of this could be captured in a magnificently designed book such as the one you now hold in your hands! Needless to say, when my publisher told me they could hire some poor wretch to type it all up for me, the deal was clinched and *The Diva Code: Miss Piggy on Life, Love, and the 10,000 Idiotic Things ~~Men~~ Frogs Do* was born!

I know what you're asking: Isn't that a bit harsh? Do men/frogs really do that many idiotic things? And isn't "idiotic" demeaning? Yes, yes, and yes, which is what makes *10,000 Idiotic Things ~~Men~~ Frogs Do . . . etc.* such a perfect subtitle.

First, the title implies a list, and everyone *adores* codes and lists! From Moses' Ten Commandments to Letterman's Top Ten, lists have always been a huge hit. They're pithy, fun, and deliciously bite-sized; kind of like a book of chocolates! Ooh, yummy!

Second, do men/frogs really do that *many* idiotic things? Oh *puh-leaze!*

Third, isn't "idiotic" a demeaning term? Well, it *can* be if one means "stupid," but I'm not using it in that way . . . or at least not *only* in that way. By saying "idiotic," I have tried to capture the rich variety of annoying, pesky, unreasonable, irrational, imbecilic, foolish, thoughtless, inconsiderate, careless, impudent, ill-mannered, cheeky, infuriating, irritating, maddening, exasperating things that men do. Obviously, no single word can say all this, but "idiotic" came up first in my thesaurus, so there you have it.

Now, lest you think this is a book of complaints, let moi assure you that I have stuffed this little volume with tons of enriching insights. Anyone who watches as much *Oprah* and *Dr. Phil* as moi can't help but be empathetic and inspiring. As you will see, *The Diva Code* offers great ideas on what vous can do to overcome the idiocies of men and frogs. And as a bonus, it will help release your inner diva, so you can get what you deserve and give others exactly what they deserve!

Yes, dearest reader, this book is moi's gift to you (not that you don't have to pay for it); it is my way of saying "thank you" for making me rich and famous . . . and here's how you can be, too!

Kissy Kissy,

Miss Piggy

A Note About the Typeface

and Other Nonsense That Didn't Fit Anyplace Else

The main text of this book is set in a typeface that was designed and named after someone whose last name sounds like one of those heavy pastries you order at a Schnitzel Hut where all the waiters wear lederhosen. Needless to say, it is a lovely typeface and I'm very happy that we chose it, but who really cares?

Now, a few words about the organization of this book.

The order of idiotic things that ~~men~~ frogs do is NOT meant to imply that some things are *more idiotic* than others. Moi believes that *all* things ~~men~~ frogs do wrong are equally idiotic, but we had to put them in some order, so live with it, sweetie.

Finally, since most—but not, by any means, all—of my relationship experience is with a certain frog, I use the terms "men" and "frogs" interchangeably throughout the book. Suffice it to say that I believe men and frogs are equally at fault. However, if you can't tell whether you're going out with a man or a frog, you have problems that are *way beyond* the purview of this book, so good luck with that.

There, I think that covers it for the time being.

You may now continue on to the good stuff.

Enjoy!
–*MP*

THE
DIVA CODE

10,000 Idiotic Things ~~Men~~ Frogs Do

1. HE'S JUST NOT READY TO COMMIT—Let's begin with one of men and frogdom's all-time idiotic offenses. You give him the pleasure of your company (plus untold hours of prep time) and in return he's not willing to commit to anything. Mention a romantic getaway, a steady and exclusive dating policy, a long-term relationship, *marriage* . . . and he runs for the exits!

> *What Vous Need to Do:* The best defense is a good offense, which means that you must never give up trying to make him commit. Remember: Never stop being offensive.

2. **HE WANTS HIS PERSONAL SPACE**—When used by men, this means he wants to keep seeing other women. (When used by women, it means she met someone cuter, so back off, buster. In her case, a perfectly reasonable request.)

> *What Vous Need to Do*: Never back off. Use his personal space for storage. One always needs extra closets.

3. **HE'S TOO FOCUSED ON HIS CAREER**—He says he's doing it for "you," so he can shower you with gifts and make you proud of his accomplishments.

> *What Vous Need to Do*: Take the gifts, but have him followed. Me thinketh he doth spend too mucheth time with hith thecretary. *(Hey, stop shpritzing and keep typing—MP)*

2

4. HE MAKES BAD CHOICES—If he didn't choose you, it's a *bad* choice.

What Vous Need to Do: Eliminate his options. From now on, you decide.

5. HE DOESN'T LISTEN—You talk and talk and talk, and he grunts "uh-huh."

What Vous Need to Do: Use this to your advantage. Once he agrees to whatever you're saying, make him sign the papers. Bingo! What's his is yours!

3

6. HE DOESN'T COMMUNICATE—Either he gives you the silent treatment or he talks and talks and talks about stuff you're not interested in.

> *What Vous Need to Do:* Continue to ignore him. Who really cares what he's yammering about, n'est pas?

7. HE IS TOO "CLINGY"—He's all over you all the time.

> *What Vous Need to Do:* Personally, I don't see this as much of a problem, but if he's really getting on your nerves, clock him with a candy dish (which you've already emptied, n'est pas?). That should give you a few pleasant, cling-free hours.

4

8. HE DOESN'T HUG, CUDDLE, COO . . . etc.—Some men and frogs have physical intimacy issues that make it difficult for them to show affection.

> *What Vous Need to Do*: Help him work through these issues, but not by exploring deep-seated psychological reasons he feels this way; get him in a headlock.

9. HE'S A HOMEBODY—Some men and frogs prefer staying home when they could be out *with vous* reveling in the social whirl and playing hide-and-seek with the paparazzi. This male behavior is not only idiotic, it's a complete waste of the new outfit you just bought.

> *What Vous Need to Do*: Take away his remote; no man can sit at home without a flipper in his flipper. He'll follow you anywhere.

5

10. **HE'S A GADABOUT**—When you want to stay home snuggling and making like turtle doves, he wants to go out gallivanting.

> *What Vous Need to Do*: Swap him for a homebody. Or live with it and live it up!

11. **HE'S GOT A BIG EGO**—Him. Him. Him. It's *always* about his wants, his needs, his concerns, his injuries, his loss of consciousness, his coma. Bor-ing!

> *What Vous Need to Do*: If he's got a big ego, *you* get a bigger one, and make him pay for it.

6

12. HE'S TOO PASSIVE—He's forever deferring to your needs and wants, rather than asserting his own opinions. You have to make all the decisions!

What Vous Need to Do: Absolutely nothing.

13. HE'S TOO AGGRESSIVE—He makes demands . . . of you. He has opinions and voices them . . . to you.

What Vous Need to Do: He has a problem . . . with you. Fight fire with fire, sister. Literally, if necessary.

14. HE'S TOO IMPULSIVE—He does things without thinking about them first. He never considers the ramifications of his actions. He's careless with his money.

> *What Vous Need to Do*: Help him . . . especially on the money part.

15. HE'S TOO CAUTIOUS—He never does anything without first conducting a cost-benefit analysis and considering its long-term impact on global warming. As a result, he lives in downtown Dullsville behind a moat, inside a wall with 24-hour armed response. Yawn!

> *What Vous Need to Do*: What are you doing with this loser? And how the heck did you get over the wall and past the guards? Throw caution to the wind . . . and him into the moat.

8

16. HE TRIES TO "FIX" THINGS—I'm not talking about home makeovers here, I'm talking about his lack of empathy and common sense. When you want him to empathize with your litany of grievances, gripes, crises, and personal problem, all he wants to do is *fix* things by offering silly solutions that will resolve your predicament. Hmph! What is he thinking!?

What Vous Need to Do: Fix him, but good.

17. HE DOESN'T TRY TO "FIX" THINGS—Now I'm talking about home makeovers.

What Vous Need to Do: Call *Extreme Makeover: Home Edition*'s Ty Pennington. He's handy with a hammer . . . and cute, too.

9

18. **HE'S TOO MACHO**—Some men insist on swaggering, asserting their masculinity as if it were some sort of banner to be waved over you, his conquest.

> *What Vous Need to Do*: Nothing deflates an overly macho ~~man~~ frog faster than making him hold your purse. Work it, girls.

19. **HE'S A WIMP**—A milquetoast who's afraid of his own shadow, and yours. Where are the swaggering, assertive, masculine men when you need them?

> *What Vous Need to Do*: Well, that's what you get for making him hold your purse.

20. HE'S STATUS OBSESSED—It's all about the label, the fancy car, the platinum-encrusted watch, the vacation place in Gstaad, the showy perks.

What Vous Need to Do: Give moi his number.

21. HE WATCHES SPORTS ALL THE TIME—The only time he stops flipping the channel is when there's yet another cockamamie sporting event where they're vying for the ultimate interplanetary world championship for the umpteenth time.

What Vous Need to Do: Learn about sports. For instance, did vous know that on some teams there are players called "tight ends"? This is worth further exploration, non?

11

22. HE'S GOT A TEMPER—Any perceived slight sends him off the deep end. He yells, screams, and throws a soon-to-be-a-major-motion-picture-sized tantrum.

What Vous Need to Do: Make it clear that his conduct is unacceptable *and* that you happen to hold the copyright on this kind of behavior, so there!

23. HE'S SECRETIVE—While you share your every feeling, insight, and advice with him, he keeps part of himself hidden away. In fact, you have to go hunting through his papers, phone records, and computer files to uncover the "real" him.

What Vous Need to Do: I don't know about you, but I enjoy spelunking for secrets. I wouldn't change a thing. If it really bothers you, try sodium pentothal.

12

24. HE'S ALWAYS JEALOUS—Your ~~man~~ frog doesn't like it when you flirt with that guy who kind of looks like Brad Pitt. (Or was it Jude Law? Oh, who cares, I wouldn't kick either one to the curb.)

> *What Vous Need to Do:* Go ahead and flirt. Your guy is going to be jealous anyway, so you might as well enjoy yourself. And if your man suddenly isn't jealous, then it's time for *you* to get jealous . . . and suspicious.

25. HE'S CODEPENDENT—Codependency was all the rage a few years back. Men who are codependent want you to make everything they do seem all right.

> *What Vous Need to Do:* If there are perks (e.g., jewelry, trips, parties, etc.), be an enabler. Otherwise, tell him to start a 12-step program and make sure his first step is out the door.

13

26. HE'S A NARCISSIST—This guy can usually be found at the gym defining his triceps, biceps, bicuspids, you name it. And when he's not pumping iron, he's primping in front of the mirror—tweezing, conditioning, moisturizing, and otherwise invading your personal grooming space.

What Vous Need to Do: Ask yourself if he's such a hunk that he's worth it. If so, get more mirrors. If not, dump him . . . but get more mirrors anyway. After all, narcissism isn't a bad thing if it's about vous.

27. HE LACKS A MORAL COMPASS—Sad to say, far too many men are simply unable to tell right from wrong.

What Vous Need to Do: Be persistent and remind him: "If moi say it, it's right; if vous say it, it's wrong."

14

28. **HE WON'T ASK FOR DIRECTIONS**—Another problem that appears to be epidemic among men, be they amphibious or otherwise.

What Vous Need to Do: Tell him where to go.

29. **HE'S GADGET OBSESSED**—If it has a screen, a battery, makes noise, and is *the absolute latest* in electronics, he will just have to run out and get one, even if he really doesn't particularly want it, need it, or know what it does.

What Vous Need to Do: Let him have his toys, but match him toy for toy. If he gets another PDA or GPS, make sure you nab another DKNY, a couple of BCBGs, with a few CKs thrown in for good measure.

15

30. HE'S UNFORGIVING—He's the kind who won't forgive a tiny faux pas, a teensy error, a minor blunder, or, on rare occasion, a great big "better-tell-our-publicist-to-start-spinning-this-one" whopper of a mistake. It's inconsiderate and, dare I say, unforgivable.

> *What Vous Need to Do*: Be infinitely patient. He'll make a mistake and you'll be ready to pounce.

31. HE DOESN'T TAKE HINTS—So many relationships are kept healthy by little hints that we women give to our men and/or frogs. Hints such as "Buy me that" or "Say 'I do.'" Yet most men are tres slow on the uptake and fail to see that we have their best interests in mind.

> *What Vous Need to Do*: Forget walking softly, time for the big stick.

16

32. **HE LIES!**—I know this is a terrible thing to infer, but we all know that some men lie. (Or was that "some of us know that all men lie"?) Either way, men will tell terrible untruths just to keep themselves from having to suffer your wrath.

> *What Vous Need to Do:* One way or the other, they're going to suffer your wrath. They might as well tell you the real reason they deserve it.

33. **HE ALWAYS HAS TO BE RIGHT**—Some men insist on "being right" even when they are obviously not. This is not merely infuriating, it's wrong!

> *What Vous Need to Do:* Treat your relationship like a game show. Tell him the judges say "sorry, you're wrong" and if he still insists on "being right" give him a nice parting gift and bring on the next contestant.

34. HE'S NOT IN TOUCH WITH HIS EMOTIONS—So many men can't cry. They repress their emotions and hold it all inside.

> *What Vous Need to Do:* As our mothers used to say—"I'll give you something to cry about." Give him a reason to cry. I'm sure you can think of something.

35. HE TURNS EVERYTHING INTO A NEGOTIATION—With this kind of man, everything (e.g., what to have for dinner, where to spend the holidays, who gets the house) must be discussed, red-lined, and endlessly haggled over.

> *What Vous Need to Do:* Call my agent, Bernie. He'll get you stuff you didn't even know you wanted.

18

36. HE ACCUSES YOU OF NAGGING—Nothing is more hurtful to a woman than when a man tells her that she nags. This is especially awful when it is obvious that she never nags, and even if she did it would be for his own good, that is if he'd only listen, which he never does, so why do we even bother?

What Vous Need to Do: Be yourself. His perceptions are his problem.

19

37. **HE'S GOT A "PETER PAN" COMPLEX**—No, I'm not talking about those round-collared shirts, which I still think look fabulous if worn with a cashmere sweater and just the right set of pearls. I'm talking about ~~men~~ frogs who refuse to grow up and want to act like little boys forever.

> *What Vous Need to Do:* Think of a wonderful thought, any merry little thought. Think of Christmas, think of snow, think of sleigh bells off you go . . . then tell him to "Grow up, buster" or he'll be flyin' all right.

38. HE'S EVASIVE—He won't answer questions or respond to friendly overtures. Heck, he's even uncooperative in front of that grand jury you were forced to convene. He always cites "some crisis" that keeps him from responding to innocent inquiries, such as: "When are we getting married, buster?"

What Vous Need to Do: Get in his face. Not only is this an effective technique for interrogation, but it's great for kissing, too.

21

39. HE GOES PLACES YOU HATE—For vous, Paris beckons, the Riviera calls your name, and Beverly Hills has you on speed dial. For him, it's some dreadful place like, oh, I don't know, say . . . the *swamp*!? It's snake-infested, rat-filled, and covered in dirty muck. Yuck! Sweetie, if I want that, I'll stay in Hollywood.

> *What Vous Need to Do:* I'm still looking into the cost of draining the swamp; I'll have to get back to you on this one.

40. HE'S FASHION CHALLENGED—One word: Green. It's all he wears. Formal, informal, casual, casual chic, urban chic, suburban chic, informal casual sub-Saharan chic . . . No matter the occasion, it's *always* the same green outfit!

> *What Vous Need to Do:* Look on the bright side—if he's naturally green, this essentially means he's not wearing anything.

22

41. **HE HAS LOSER FRIENDS**—Oh sure, it was fine for him to hang out with blue-nosed chicken-dating weirdos, pun-impaired bears, conniving shrimp, and assorted other pests *before* he met *you*. But he's met you and they're still around . . . and they *never go away!*

> *What Vous Need to Do:* Beats me. I've tried everything on this one. If you have any ideas, let me know pronto!

42. **HE'S A FROG WHO DOESN'T REALIZE HOW FORTUNATE HE IS TO HAVE MOI, AND OUGHTA BE GLAD I PUT UP WITH HIS . . .**

> . . . Hold on! I'm not typing any more of this. I quit!–K the F

Dearest Reader,

How was moi to know that the publisher would hire Kermie to type up my book? And now, for some cockamamie reason, Kermie is mad about what I've written. He shouldn't be. After all, moi didn't mention him by name. (My lawyer said that was a big "no-no".) But, hey frog, if the shoe fits, well ... you know the rest.

It's true that moi promised vous "10,000 Idiotic Things ~~Men~~ Frogs Do." And I shall deliver. However, since I have no intention of typing this stuff up myself, there are two things you can do:

Go to www.Muppets.com and look for the rest of the list. It's not there, but I get a nickel a head for every warm body I drive to the site, so visit there, pretty please! Or you can ...

Be industrious and create your own list of 9,958 other idiotic things with the following Idiotic List Template.

— *Idiotic List Template* —

He (*Describe Idiotic Behavior Here*)—First he (*List Annoyances Here in Ascendingly Infuriating Order*), then he (*Secondary Grievances Here*), and as if that weren't enough he (*Tertiary, Forthiary, and Fifthtiary Gripes Here*).

What Vous Need to Do: I always
(*Threats and Consequences Here*).

Fabulously simple, non?! Once you complete your list, you'll be ready to bask in moi's life-changing insights, soak up my celebrity wisdom, and get in touch with your inner Diva!

So don't just sit there, read on . . . Or better yet, let some gorgeous guy read it to you while feeding you chocolates. 'Tis bliss!

Kissy Kissy,
Miss Piggy

· 1 ·

Awaken the Diva Within

Everything You Always Wanted to Know
About Being a Diva . . .
But Were Far Too Important to Ask

What Every Diva Needs to Know . . .

It is better to live

beyond your means

than beneath your standards.

What Every Diva Needs to Know . . .

Too much is never enough.

What Every Diva Needs to Know ...

When the going gets tough,

vous are obviously in the wrong place.

What Every Diva Needs to Know ...

If at first you don't succeed,

complain loudly until they give it to you.

What Every Diva Needs to Know . . .

Anything worth doing is worth having
someone do for you.

What Every Diva Needs to Know . . .

Never put off until tomorrow
what you can buy today.

Diva Dos...

Always be generous
. . . to yourself.

Always be gracious.
You never know who's going to marry into money.

Always forgive and forget.
(Except in cases where total and complete
annihilation of your adversary is the only logical
option, which happens more often than vous might
imagine.)

Always be 100 percent sincere.
No really, I mean it . . . Honestly.
Would moi lie to vous?

31

Diva Don'ts...

Never fly coach. Never fly commercial.
And most of all, never fly with Gonzo.

Never do an infomercial,
unless they throw in the beachfront place in Maui
where it's being shot.

Never say "no" to a charity,
especially if it's for a good cause,
and most especially if you get to buy a new dress
and sit next to George Clooney.

Never use your position of power to harm others,
unless they obviously deserve it.

Never hold a grudge.
Act on it.

Never *ever* touch my frog.

What Makes a Diva...

Being a diva is *not* about your money,

looks, status, and fabulous accessories.

It is about your personal commitment to excellence

and

your money, looks, status, and fabulous accessories.

What Else Makes a Diva...

Being a diva is *not* about

hyperventilating rants,

over-the-top temper tantrums,

and outrageous demands.

(. . . Oh wait, yes it is.)

33

Diva Words to Live By . . .

The best things in life are free
. . . if you get comped.

If you can't stand the heat
. . . turn up the air conditioning.

The bucks stop here.

You can lead a horse to water,
but why would you want to?

If you can dream it,
you can marry it.

Let moi eat cake!

Fame vs. Obscurity

Fame wins.

Dealing with Paparazzi

They can make you look bad, so make them look good.

If they start getting obnoxious and in-your-face,
simply yell "amateur" and show them how the pros do it.

Be friendly. Offer them refreshments.
Send them holiday cards.
Find out where they live, then
stalk them relentlessly and see how they like it.

If you're really in a hurry,
learn to run backward smiling.

Never be rude.
That's what publicists are for.

Can vous say:
"Hiiiiiiii-yaaaaaaaaa!!!"

36

Becoming a Diva

Be yourself.

Believe in yourself.

Get an entourage.

Get your entourage to believe in you.

Get a publicist.

Pay your publicist to believe in you.

Get your publicist to figure out how to get other people to believe in you *without* paying them.

Rinse and repeat.

When a Diva Meets a Diva...

Air kissing. Not just a good idea.
It's the law.

If you don't know who they are, just remember:
Everyone's first name is "Darling!"

Hey, if they got this close to you,
they must be somebody.

Always make sure this person is *not* the person that
you're dishing about before you start dishing about
someone who's not here.
(Ew! Awkward.)

In case of emergency:
Talk shoes.

38

Celebrity and Royalty and Diva

A diva is somewhere between

a celebrity and a member of royalty.

If that diva is moi,

she's *right* in between, smiling at the camera.

Diva Dining Out

You are where you eat.

Diva Work Ethic

Those who can, do.

Those who can have someone else do it

are moi's kind of people.

39

The Way of the Diva

Surround yourself
with people who want to be vous.

Get in touch with your inner diva,
Even if it means leaving a message with her service.

Embrace scandal.
Embarrassment is a small price for publicity.

Make a grand entrance.
(No grand, no entrance.)

Don't just count your blessings,
have them audited regularly.

Demand as much of yourself
as you do of others.
Naaah!

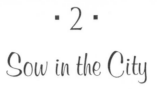

· 2 ·

Sow in the City

A Singular Single Girl's Look at Love

Finding Love

Love turns up where you least expect it.

So look there first.

What Is Love?

Love is a special feeling between two people.

(Between a pig and a frog, it's *wowee-wow-wow!*)

What Is Lust?

Lust is love minus the paperwork.

What Is the Difference Between Love and Lust?

About three expensive dinners
and some oversized jewelry.

43

How to Tell If He's into You

He can't take his eyes off of you,
even when you're not playing three-card monte
for his platinum wristwatch.

He whispers sweet nothings in your ear
without making you remove your iPod.

He speaks your name lovingly . . .
even though you haven't the foggiest idea who he is.

He gets down on his knee, pledges eternal love, and
offers you a diamond ring.
(Or so I've heard.)

How to Tell If He's NOT into You

He says: "I'm NOT into you . . .
now please go back to your own table
before Angelina gets here."

When you suggest seeing each other again,
he pulls out a blindfold.

He can't take his eyes off of you . . .
but only to make sure you're not following
as he makes his escape.

He remembers your name, your face, and the car you
were driving when you tried to run him over as he
made his escape.

He has the restraining order against you
tattooed on his chest.

45

Men vs. Women
Women win.

46

Before You Go Out with Him

Ask Yourself . . .

Is he my type?

(Check all that apply)

❑ Cute / ❑ Rich / ❑ Human / ❑ Amphibian /

❑ Other

If he canceled, would I be . . .

❑ Devastated / ❑ Disappointed / ❑ Relieved /

❑ Ecstatic

When this date is over will I be . . .

❑ In love / ❑ Incensed / ❑ In traction

47

Before You Marry Him
Ask Yourself . . .

Who is this person?

Never mind spending the rest of my life with him,
can I make it through this boring conversation?

How do I get this diamond to a jeweler for an appraisal
before telling him "yes" or "no"?

Would seeing me without my makeup kill him
. . . and is this a bad thing?

Is he green and does he belong to someone else?

48

The Stages of Dating

1. Looking for Mr. Right.

2. Looking for Mr. Right Now.

3. Looking for Mr. All Right
   But Needs Some Work.

4. Looking for Mr. Wrong
   Because You're Sure You Can Change
   Him into Mr. Right.

5. Right? Wrong? Who cares? I'll take him!

49

Dating: Phone Etiquette

Never call him.

Never call him back.

Never call him "You moronic chucklehead."

Never answer on the first ring.

Never answer
  . . . then conference him in with all the other guys
you're dating.

50

First Date Etiquette

Never be ready for him when he arrives . . .
but always get to him before he escapes.

Don't just talk about yourself.
Let him talk about you, too.

Show you're interested in what he has to say
by occasionally listening and interjecting witty
rejoinders, such as:

> "Uh-huh," "Yeah, sure," and "Does this story
> have a point?"

End the first date early.
Remember: You've got two other first dates scheduled
for tonight.

First Date Romantic Quotient:
A kiss on the cheek is appropriate.

51

Second Date Etiquette

Try to figure out which one he is.

Let him to talk about himself.
(This may help you figure out which one he is.)

Do a credit and background check.

Watch *America's Most Wanted* and
make sure he's not the lead story.

Get his PIN number.

Show him you are independent by offering to pick up
the check.
(If he accepts this offer, pick it up, hand it to him, and leave.)

Be coy.
The attitude, not the fish.

52

Second Date Romantic Quotient:
A kiss and a chaste embrace are appropriate.

Third Date Etiquette

At this point it's okay for both of you to remove the "Hello! My Name Is . . ." stickers.

Don't answer your cell phone during the date
. . . unless of course it's one of your girlfriends wanting to know how the date is going.

Suggest you go someplace different tonight.
Like . . . oh, say . . . a jewelry store!

Must-haves: A notary public and a prenup.

Remember: Vegas is open all night!

Third Date Romantic Quotient:
Appropriate shmappropriate. Use your imagination!

The Art of Flirting

DO bat your eyelashes.
DON'T hit him with a bat.

DO show him your smile.
DON'T bite him.

DO talk about yourself.
DON'T do a PowerPoint presentation.

DO write down your phone number.
DON'T write it on his forehead.

DO ask about his past.
DON'T hire a private investigator (yet).

DO flirt with other men.
DON'T let another woman near him.

54

Jealousy

They say jealousy is the green-eyed monster.

There is a reason for this.

And trust moi, vous don't want to know it.

55

He Asked for It...

What to Say When You Feel Like Fighting

Does this dress make me look fat?

Should I buy these shoes?

Mind if we watch the figure skating competition?

Mind if I drive?

The remote? Oh, I threw that out.

56

Types of Dating

SERIAL DATING

More than one date per night.

RECREATIONAL DATING

Dating for sport, not sustenance.

MULTITASK DATING

Dating while doing more important things like your
nails, your taxes, updating Facebook, updating your face.

DOUBLE DATING

Two men. One restaurant.

(Ideally one with large plants and wide pillars—
the restaurant, not the men.)

PROMOTIONAL DATING

Going out with someone to publicize your new movie,
album, website, or line of designer hair-care products.

CARBON DATING

Going out with someone *a lot older* than you.

MISTAKE DATING

Going out and not coming back.

57

Breaking Up . . .

A User's Guide to Getting Out After Going Out

EASY

You both agree to go your own way.

> WHAT TO SAY: *"Good-bye and good luck!"*

GRACEFUL

You go your own way . . . and he gives you an expensive parting gift.

> WHAT TO SAY: *"Hmm, on second thought . . ."*

AWKWARD

You go your own way . . . and he doesn't notice you're gone.

> WHAT TO SAY: *"That's the last time I date a dead guy."*

CREEPY

You go your own way . . . and he follows.

> WHAT TO SAY: *"Go ahead, make moi's day."*

VENGEFUL

You say you're going . . . but you stay.

> WHAT TO SAY: *"Nobody gets rid of moi that easy, buster!"*

· 3 ·

~~Men~~ Frogs Are from the Swamp, Women Are from the Spa

Why They're Always Wrong and You're Always Right

Variations on a Theme

Men are from donuts,
women are from pastry carts.

Men are from the rodeo,
women are from Rodeo Drive.

Men are from Mars,
women are from Godiva.

Why Women Care About Chocolate and Shoes
Duh!

Why Men Care About Gadgets
Dumb.

Men: Common Consumer Complaints

Some Assembly Required.

Does Not Follow Directions.

Does Not Come with Directions.

Does Not Ask for Directions.

May Not Be Available
with Desired Options.

Built-in Obsolescence.

Long-Term Service Contract
Is Worthless.

All Sales Final.

Men:
What They Say and What They Mean

What They Say . . .

"Shall we dance?"

"Are you doing anything Saturday?"

"Would you like dessert?"

"May I escort you home?"

"No, I don't want to come up, but thanks for asking."

"I'll call."

What They Mean . . .

"You look good enough to show my friends."

"Or are you a loser like me?"

"Please say no! I've already spent $300 on dinner!"

"Oh boy oh boy oh boy!"

"Do I have to slow the car down? Or can you jump out now?"

"Bwah-hahahahahaha!"

63

Women:
What They Say and What They Mean

What They Say . . .	What They Mean . . .
"I've never met anyone quite like you before."	"And I hope I never do again."
"Do you come here often?"	"I want to know if it's safe to ever come back"
"Dance with you? I'd love to!"	"As long as you face the other way and count to ten."
"I'm not seeing anyone now."	"That includes you."
"Go out on Saturday?"	"What year?"
"Come up to your place?"	"In your dreams, buster!"
"Would I like to go out again?"	"Yes. Right now. And with someone else."
"Oh, you'll call moi?"	"Bwah-hahahahahahaha!"

64

Definitions:
Everything a Woman Needs to Know About . . .

Football—Tight ends, offsides, and holding.
What's not to like?

Baseball—A-Rod. Cute . . . and very rich.

Basketball—Men in silk boxers getting sweaty.

Golf—Tiger Woods . . . and a bunch of other guys.

Definitions:
Everything a Man Needs to Know About . . .

Shoes—More, yes! Too many, never.

Chocolate—See "Shoes."

Jewelry—See "Chocolate."

Shopping—See "Jewelry."

Understanding Men

Everything you need to know about men you learn in kindergarten:

They miss Mommy.

They like to tease.

They throw tantrums.

They love snack time.

They pick their nose.

And they need their nap.

Understanding Women

Everything you need to know about
women you learn at the sales rack.

They want what they want
They want it right now.
They want what they can't have.
They want it with matching shoes.
They didn't want it until they saw you had it.
They know exactly what it is they want . . .
and this isn't it.

Making Change

There Are Two Ways to Change a Man . . .

THE HARD WAY

. . . Change his appearance (e.g., hairstyle, wardrobe, etc.)

. . . Change his behavior (e.g., lifestyle, habits, etc.)

. . . Change his demeanor (e.g., attitude, appreciation for vous, etc.)

THE EASY WAY

. . . Exchange him.

~~MEN~~ FROGS ARE FROM THE SWAMP . . .

Why Women Are Superior to Men

Women listen to women.
Men don't.

Women learn from their mistakes.
Men marry theirs.

Women have babies.
Men are babies.

Moi is a woman.
Game. Set. Match.

· 4 ·

Some Like It Haute

Dressing for Excess

Moi's Fashion Credo

If it's expensive, it fits.

What Your Clothes Say About You...

Clothes are the welcome mat

at the doorway to romance.

Make sure your clothes say:

"Come in! Moi is expecting vous!"

Not:

"Scram!"

Some of Moi's Favorite Designers
BCBG, DKNY, CK

... and if there's any money left,

I buy a few vowels.

73

On Looking Your Best...

Wear clothes that are distinct, elegant,
and—if you're dating a frog—waterproof.

Wear flattering clothes.
If this is not possible, surround yourself
with people who will flatter you
no matter what clothes you're wearing.

Soak in a hot tub twice a day
. . . preferably with someone rich and handsome.

Diamonds are best,
but in sufficient number, any high-priced gemstone
ain't bad.

Everyone looks better when they're draped in green.
(Hands off the frog, sister!)

Moi's Fashion Insight, Part Un

Cognoscenti, fashionistas, and paparazzi are not pasta entrees.

❧

Moi on Style

Style is about being yourself.
This works gangbusters if you happen to be moi.
If not, just hope for the best.

Style is about expressing your inner self,
capturing your personal ethos,
and spending someone else's money.

Being stylish begins with loving who you are.
If you have trouble loving who you are,
may I suggest loving who I am?

Being stylish is lots of work:
You must constantly
maintain your image, update your look,
and destroy old photos that show you
wearing spandex and big hair.

Style comes in all shapes and sizes.
The bigger you are, the more style you have.

Designers and Moi

The fashion world looks to moi for inspiration.

I look to the fashion world for freebies.

Making a Fashion Statement

I like moi's clothes to make a statement.

Preferably I want them to say:

"Hey, look at me,

I'm wearing really expensive clothes!"

77

Today's Most Annoying Fashions

Hip Huggers

If moi wants my hips hugged, I'll call the frog.

Leggings

They look fabulous, but getting them on and off usually
requires a winch, a block & tackle, and a
visit to moi's chiropractor.

Body Piercing

Moi prefers to skewer *others*.

Too-Tight T-shirts

I prefer clothes that breathe
. . . or at least allow *moi* to breathe.

Moi's Fashion Insight, Part Deux
Clothes are like friends:
They should always compliment
your appearance.

🌸

79

Dressing for Yourself

When it comes to dressing, I believe in
pleasing myself first.
Only then do I worry about pleasing others
. . . but not as if they really mattered.

Moi believes in dressing for myself.
Otherwise, it gets too crowded in the dressing room.

Always be yourself.
That way you won't have to get everything
monogrammed again and again.

How can one possibly dress for others?
What if you don't all wear the same size?

Celebrity Fashion

Incognito Ergo Sum.

I dress like a celebrity,

Therefore I must be one.

How to Dress Like You're Rich...
Spend lots of money.

How to Dress Like You're Rich and Smart...

Spend lots of someone else's money.

How to Tell If You Are a Fashion Victim...

When you go to an art gallery,
you are frequently mistaken for an installation.

When you go to Las Vegas,
it's assumed that you lost the bet.

When you enter a room, people don't just gasp
. . . oxygen masks drop from the ceiling.

When you go to a designer's trunk show,
you leave in the trunk.

Conjugating Fashion
   Your money
   Their money
   Armani
   ❧

· 5 ·

Extreme Makeover: Moi Edition

Beauty, Health, Fitness, and Vous

Moi's #1 Beauty Secret

Start out perfect

. . . and don't change a thing.

Moi's Recipe for Success

If you are what you eat,

. . . then eat what you love

and you'll always love yourself!

86

More of Moi's Beauty Secrets

Keep your looks the way moi does:
In jars on your dressing table.

Accentuate your best features
by pointing at them.

Conceal your flaws
by sucker punching anyone who mentions them.

Liposuction and chocolate.
Not in that order.

Hang out with weirdos.
You'll look fabulous by comparison.

87

Moi on Chocolate . . . and Visa Versa

Think of chocolate
as an accessory
for your hips.

More on Chocolate

I like my chocolate
the way I like my men:
So rich you want to marry it.

Moi on Dieting

Never eat anything you can't lift.

Lucky for moi,

I can bench-press a pastry cart.

Moi Favorite Diet...

Miss Piggy's Rich Food Diet

It doesn't matter what food you eat,

as long as somebody rich pays for it.

89

Moi on Cosmetic Surgery

Moi has *never* had a little work done.
A ton of work, sure . . . but never a little.

In fact, if moi has any more work done,
they may have to unionize my face.

When discussing cosmetic surgery,
moi prefers the term "upgraded."
Right now, you're looking at
"Miss Piggy: Version 17.8."

You know you've had too many face-lifts
when they send you a free membership in the
Surgical Mask of the Month Club.

What's the point of looking in the mirror
if vous can't surprise yourself?

90

Getting Fit Without Having a Fit

Hire personal trainers
and let them work out for you.
After all, they're getting paid, not you.

Take up a physically challenging hobby
such as rock climbing, hiking, or outlet-mall shopping.

Buy an at-home fitness machine for your bedroom.
After about two weeks, get a major workout
looking for it under all those dirty clothes.

Set up a daily workout regimen.
Look at it daily.

Work on all major muscle groups,
especially the cute ones who hang out
down at the gym.

If all else fails:
Letterbox your mirrors.

The Importance of Health

Moi believes that nothing is
more important than your health.*

*Except, of course, fame, wealth, publicity, high-profile
celebrity shmoozing, loaner jewelry for awards shows, designer
swag bags, contractual final cut, points on the gross, and
Kermie.

Moi on Aging

Like a bottle of wine,

a woman's appearance improves with age.

Hmm, come to think of it,

a woman's appearance also improves

with a bottle of wine.

Aging Is Easy

Moi doesn't mind getting older,

I just don't see the point.

· 6 ·

Rich Moi, Famous Moi

What the Rich and Famous
Know About Money and Careers—
That the Penniless and Obscure Do Not!

Career Tip #1: Ambition

Ambition is what drives us.
Marrying wealthy is what
provides the driver.

Career Tip #2: The Glass Ceiling

The only thing more difficult than breaking
the Glass Ceiling
is finding someone to sweep up the shards.

Career Tip #3: Job vs. Career

People who work to live have a "job."
People who live to work have a "career."
People who have people do all the work for them
have it made.

Economics 101

Having money is not important.

Spending money is.

Satisfaction Guaranteed

Work well done is its own reward

. . . at least that's what I tell my staff.

97

Choosing a Career

1. Decide what you like to do.

2. Get paid for it.

Job Seeking Dos and Don'ts

Successful Job Seeking Campaigns for Moi . . .

Miss Piggy
She Had You at Hiiiiii-Yaaaaa!!!

Miss Piggy
Because Everyone Else Is Just Someone Else

Miss Piggy
Now with More Moi!

Miss Piggy
. . . Obviously

The #1 On-the-Job Rule

Never ever under any circumstances whatsoever become romantically involved with someone you work with.*

Does NOT apply to pigs and frogs.

Being a Good Boss

Treat others the way they are
contractually obligated
to treat you.

The Secret of Not Getting Fired

Do nothing wrong.
Do nothing.

101

The Riddle of Fame

If a celebrity falls into a scandal,

and doesn't get press coverage,

are they still a celebrity?

102

How to Become Famous

1. DO SOMETHING IMPORTANT.

   (Alternate: *Marry, date, or just happen to be in the same picture with someone famous; or do something foolish and immature; or say something outrageous; or wear something outrageous; or get outraged by something that someone said or wore, etc.*)

2. HIRE A PUBLICIST.

103

Test Your Celebritude

Do You Have What It Takes to Be a Celebrity?

1. Are you ready to make any sacrifice to realize your goal, and if so, who exactly are you willing to sacrifice?

2. Are you willing to devote your life to seeking the approval of people you don't know, who seem to have nothing better to do than wonder if vous and the Celebrity Flavor of the Week are really a hot item?

3. Are you allergic to paparazzi?

4. When another celebrity suffers a scandal, would you feel: (A) sorry, (B) relieved, (C) delighted, (D) jealous, or (E) all of the above.

5. If you were a tree, what kind of tree would you be?

6. If vous—an A-list star—were accidentally introduced to a B-list star, would you: (A) be gracious and polite, (B) excuse yourself and call security, (C) pretend you were invisible, (D) feign a coma, or (E) all of the above.

7. Does Oprah know vous?

8. Does moi know vous?

9. If you answered Question 5, why?

10. Did you have an assistant fill this out for vous? (Ooh, marvelous! You're on your way to celebritude!)

What Being Famous Means to Moi . . .

The joy of being known by a single syllable:
Moi!

Getting into places no one can get into.

Being the reason no one can get into those places.

Being recognized by moi's fans.

Having bodyguards to keep away fans who recognize
moi.

Meeting moi's fellow celebrities
. . . and finding them wanting.

Meeting moi's fellow celebrities
. . . and finding them wanting my autograph.

Kermie.
Sure, he would love moi even if I wasn't famous.
But I am, so there!

On Fame, Fortune, and Amphibians

Fame and fortune are fabulous.

And moi highly recommends them both.

But what truly matters to moi is love.

For without love, accolades and wealth signify nothing.

. . . Well, okay, not *nothing* . . .

I mean, they're pretty good by themselves.

In fact, they're gangbusters!

Besides, being a celebrity means moi can have it all!

Fame, fortune . . . and the frog!

Ooh, sometimes I just *adore* being moi!

107

Piggy Power

Seeking Your Inner Vous;
Showing Off Your Outer Moi

On Self-Help

Moi strongly believes in self-help.
Wherever I am, I help myself to
whatever I can.

Pathway to Happiness

Open up. Look inside.
Let your inner light shine forth.
If nothing looks fresh or inviting,
order takeout.

Learning to Love Yourself

Love yourself just as you are.
Failing this, might I suggest
identity theft?

Embrace Change

Change is good,

especially if it involves a great deal of accessorizing.

Changing Others

Vous cannot force others to change.

However, vous can make them

extremely uncomfortable

until they come around to

your way of thinking.

Taking Control of Your Life
Self-discipline:
Once vous can outsource this,
everything else is easy.

Taking Control of Others' Lives
Always ask yourself:
Who am I to say how others
should live their lives?
Then go ahead and
take over.

112

Transforming Yourself: 12-Step Program

1. Admit you need to change.

2. Decide what you want to change into.

3. Conduct a personal inventory.

4. Discover that you have nothing.

5. Make a list of all those who can help you.

6. Reach out to everyone on your list.

7. Seek their advice and availability.

8. Accept their best offer.

9. Assume responsibility for deciding where to go and what to do.

10. Actively participate in your transformation.

11. Contemplate your achievement over lunch.

12. Admit you want to change again.

13. Rinse and repeat.

113

Transforming Yourself: 3-Step Program
(Microwave Version)

1. Admit you need to change.
2. Decide what you want to change into.
3. Buy it.

Self-Discovery

Of course moi is in touch with
my inner child.
Can I help it if the kid likes to
throw tantrums?

Grow and Learn

Vous May Have Problems If . . .

. . . The only way you can get in touch with
your personal feelings is via BlackBerry.

. . . When bad things happen to good people,
you can't remember which side you're rooting for.

. . . You have a condition named after you.

. . . There's a fly in your "Chicken Soup for the Soul."

. . . Dr. Phil throws up his hands
and says, "You're nuts!"

115

· 8 ·

To Have and Have More

Curtain Calls, Encores, and Other Parting Shots

Moi on Awards

Moi believes that

Hollywood gives too many awards

. . . to other people.

For Your Consideration (in _All_ categories): Moi!

Why hasn't moi won an Oscar?

Oh, I'm sure there are many reasons. The Academy can be so fickle, and then there's professional jealousy because of moi's superior acting chops (don't even think of making a joke about that), and there's personal jealousy because moi is so effortlessly and elegantly beautiful. And then, there's the whole matter of Kermie; so many actresses wish he were theirs. (Sorry, sister, you may get the little gold guy, but the little green one is moi's.) And finally, though I hate to mention it, there's the species-ism. Ever notice how people seem to win every year? Hmm?

Never a pig nor frog?

(Okay, occasionally a rat wins, but whaddaya expect, it's Hollywood.)

Is this a coincidence? Hah! More like conspiracy! But, as it is, I don't give the matter a lot of thought. It's out of moi's control . . . at least for now.

119

Moi on Getting a Lifetime Achievement Award

Oh, moi would be honored to accept such an award. But I don't think it's fair to the Academy. Lifetime Achievement always feels like an award they give because they feel bad about not giving you a real award sooner. Why feel bad later, sweetie?! Gimme the real thing now and we'll all be happy, n'est pas?

120

Moi on Overcoming Fear

Has moi ever been afraid?

Of course!

Everyone must overcome fear.

I used to be afraid of failing or looking foolish.

Now I'm not.

. . . Afraid, I mean.

Or failed.

Or foolish.

. . . Next question!

Moi on "The Relationship"

Kermie and moi's relationship

is as strong as ever:

Moi loves him.

He loves moi.

And moi love moi.

Moi on Hollywood Romance

Kermit and moi have just become
the longest-running interspecies couple in show business.
And, in Hollywood, the competition in that category is
more intense than vous might imagine.

Moi on "The Marriage Question"

Kermie and moi are married in our hearts.
I'm still working on the rest of him.

On Technical Difficulties

Technically speaking,
Kermie and moi are not *married*, per se.
But speaking spiritually, psychically,
financially, vous name it . . .
. . . the frog and the pig are hitched.

122

On Future Projects

I promise vous this:

Moi's next project is going to be bigger than *Titanic*!

The movie . . . not the boat.

123

On Near Misses

Most people don't realize that

moi was *this close* to winning the Nobel Prize.

Who could possibly have known

Global Warming would beat Creative Accessorizing

as the hot-button issue of the moment?

On Having Any Regrets

Moi doesn't have any regrets.
Instead, I have very thorough
publicists, lawyers, and film editors.

On Final Words

Last words? That's easy:
"Back off, buster!
I've still got two encores and a curtain call!"

125

Why Kermit Matters

Kermie makes moi possible.

Impossible, I can do myself.